Modern US Navy & Marine Corps Aircraft

MW00715700

Aboard the aircraft carrier USS *Carl Vinson* (CVN 70) in the Sea of Japan, March 2003, an F/A-18C Hornet is carefully guided on to a catapult by an Aircraft Director prior to it being launched.

US AIR POWER

Modern US Navy & Marine Corps Aircraft

Aircraft, Weapons and their Battlefield Might

Anthony A. Evans

Greenhill Books
LONDON

Stackpole Books
PENNSYLVANIA

Greenhill Books

Modern US Navy & Marines Corps Aircraft
first published 2004 by Greenhill Books,
Lionel Leventhal Limited, Park House, 1 Russell Gardens,
London NW11 9NN
www.greenhillbooks.com
and
Stackpole Books, 5067 Ritter Road, Mechanicsburg,
PA 17055, USA

British Library Cataloguing in Publication Data

Evans, Anthony A.
Modern US Navy & Marine Corps aircraft: aircraft,
weapons and their battlefield might. – (US air power: the
illustrated history of American air power, the campaigns,
the aircraft and the men)

1. United States. Navy – Aviation – Equipment and
supplies
2. United States. Marine Corps – Aviation – Equipment
and supplies
3. Airplanes, Military – United States
4. United States – History, Naval – 20th century
I. Title
359.9'4834'0973'09045

ISBN 1-85367-629-2

*Library of Congress Cataloging in Publication Data
available*

Designed by DAG Publications Ltd
Layout by Anthony A. Evans
Printed in Singapore

MODERN US NAVY & MARINE CORPS AIRCRAFT

'Where is the nearest carrier?' This is the first question the President of the United States of America always asks whenever faced with an overseas military dilemma.

US Navy and Marine Corps air power is the epitome of US power projection – the aircraft carrier's worldwide ability to operate in international waters means that its aircraft do not need to secure landing rights on any foreign soil. Each carrier and its air wing provides a mini airforce that can be rushed to any potential trouble spot with the minimum of delay, worldwide. If the leader of a hostile country suddenly finds he has a US carrier and its Battle Group parked off his country's shores, he knows he's in trouble. A typical example of this was during the early part of 1998. Iraq refused to allow UN weapons inspectors to investigate certain sites that were suspected of being involved in the production of weapons of mass destruction. The nuclear-powered carrier USS *John C. Tennis* immediately sailed from her base in Virginia to the coast of Iraq in less than thirteen days (8,000 nautical miles), her average speed being over 25 knots. When she arrived off the Iraqi coast Saddam suddenly complied with the inspectors' requests.

The US Navy operates some 4,000 aircraft, both from land and from the sea. As well as operating from mighty aircraft carriers and amphibious warfare ships, aircraft can be seen on cruisers, destroyers and frigates, and also aboard the 'glamour-less', but very vital, auxiliary supply or replenishment ships.

The US Marine Corps has a large air arm which is separate to that of the Navy, but is very closely aligned to it. Its main role is the support of ground forces during an amphibious landing and when the troops are established ashore. The Marine Corps operates the full range of aircraft types: combat fixed-wing aircraft, combat helicopters, assault helicopters, transports and electronic warfare planes.

The aircraft carrier functions as the centrepiece of an Aircraft Carrier Battle Group and is supported by the other combat ships in the Group, as well as by supply vessels. Typically the Group consists of the carrier and possibly two guided-missile cruisers, which each have a powerful multi-mission capability, including Tomahawk long-range cruise missiles. Also there is a guided-missile destroyer, which is well able to defend against enemy surface combatants and hostile warplanes, plus an anti-submarine destroyer and an anti-submarine frigate. There are also two nuclear-powered attack submarines which are used in a direct support role, seeking out and destroying enemy combat ships and submarines. Within the Group there is also a combined ammunition, oiler and supply ship, providing logistic support for the warships.

At present there are five US fleets. The US Second Fleet's operational area is the whole of the Atlantic Ocean. The Third Fleet is responsible for the central and eastern Pacific. The Fifth Fleet operates in the Red Sea, the Arabian Sea and the Persian Gulf, and has been very much in the news during the last few years. The Sixth Fleet's operational area is the Mediterranean, and the Seventh Fleet's is the western Pacific and the Indian Ocean.

The US Navy has twelve massive aircraft carriers. These are:

USS *Ronald Reagan* (CVN 76)
USS *Harry S. Truman* (CVN 75)
USS *John C. Stennis* (CVN 74)
USS *George Washington* (CVN 73)
USS *Abraham Lincoln* (CVN 72)
USS *Theodore Roosevelt* (CVN 71)
USS *Carl Vinson* (CVN 70)
USS *Dwight D. Eisenhower* (CVN 69)
USS *Nimitz* (CVN 68)
USS *John F. Kennedy* (CV 67)
USS *Enterprise* (CVN 65)
USS *Kitty Hawk* (CV 63)

Ten are nuclear powered – each displacing in the region of 100,000 tons when fully loaded – and 1,000 feet or so in length. There are two more nuclear-powered carriers in the planning stages. The two conventionally powered carriers, the USS *John F. Kennedy* and USS *Kitty Hawk,* are over 80,000 tons displacement. These powerful ships can be used for anything from simply showing the US flag and displaying a powerful presence in any area of the world to attacking hostile enemy aircraft, ships and shore targets. The Aircraft Carrier Battle Group is also well able to make the ultimate threat, the use of nuclear weapons. The aircraft carrier therefore provides a huge range of options for the US government in both peace and war.

The Carrier Replacement Program provides for the construction of new aircraft carriers. At present, of the twelve active carriers in the US fleet, nine are of the *Nimitz* class. In January 2001 Newport News Shipbuilding was awarded the contract to build the last *Nimitz*-class carrier, CVN 77, and it is scheduled to be delivered in March 2008.

Each carrier operates an air wing of between 80 and 90 aircraft. The typical air wing consists of three F/A-18 Hornet squadrons, one F-14 Tomcat squadron, one EA-6B Prowler squadron, one S-3 Viking squadron, one E-2C Hawkeye squadron, and one H-60 Seahawk squadron, and has a mix of Navy and Marine Corps squadrons operating together.

Aircraft combat squadrons are also operated from a dozen or so amphibious-warfare ships. These ships superficially loo like aircraft carriers, weighing in approximately 40,000 tons and being ov 750 feet in length. Their air groups, howeve cannot operate fixed-wing aircraft except fo the V/STOL Harrier, although they ca operate a mix of helicopters and Harrier depending on the mission requirements. Th seven *Wasp*-class helicopter/dock-landir ships and the five *Tarawa*-class amphibiou assault ships normally operate twelve CH-4 Sea Knight and four CH-53 Super Stallic helicopters, six AV-8B Harriers, four AH-1 Super Cobra ground-attack helicopters, plu three UH-1 Huey utility helicopters. Variou other amphibious and dock-landing ships ca also accommodate the whole range of Nav and Marine Corps helicopters.

Cruisers, destroyers, frigates and flee supply ships all have a wide-rangir helicopter capability. The *Ticonderoga*-cla cruisers have a twin hangar and a flight-dec and are capable of operating two SH-60 Seahawk ASW helicopters. The *Arleigh Burk* class destroyers are able to operate wit helicopters as they have a flight-deck, b they do not have a hangar, so they can on temporarily operate with them, n accommodate them. The most recent ships the class have been built with a hangar fo two helicopters, and as such they have permanent complement of two Seahawks. Th *Spruance*-class destroyers have a helicopt hangar and are able to accommodate on aircraft. The *Oliver Hazard Perry*-clas frigates have a twin hangar and are able operate two Seahawk ASW helicopters. Th Navy cargo ships and supply vessels all hav helicopter flight-deck facilities, some with hangar. For example, the AOE-class fas combat support ships have a hangar that ca accommodate three large twin-rotor Se Knight helicopters.

US Navy and Marine Corps Squadron Prefixes

The US Secretary of the Navy, in July 192 decided to standardise nomenclature for classes and types of US Navy vessels ar aircraft. Lighter-than-air aircraft we identified by the letter 'Z' and heavier-than-a

HC	Helicopter Combat Support Squadron	VF	Fighter Squadron
HCS	Helicopter Combat Support Special Squadron	VFA	Strike Fighter Squadron
HM	Helicopter Mine Countermeasures Squadron	VFC	Fighter Squadron Composite
HMA	Helicopter Marine Attack Squadron	VFP	Light Photo Reconnaissance Squadron
HMH	Helicopter Marine Heavy Transport Squadron	VMA	Marine Attack Squadron
HMLA	Helicopter Marine Light Attack Squadron	VMAT	Marine Attack Training Squadron
HMM	Helicopter Marine Medium Transport Squadron	VMAQ	Marine Attack/Electronic Warfare Squadron
HMX	Helicopter Marine Experimental Squadron	VMFA	Marine Fighter/Attack Squadron
HS	Helicopter Antisubmarine Squadron	VMFAT	Marine Fighter/Attack Training Squadron
HSL	Helicopter Antisubmarine Squadron (Light)	VMFP	Marine Fighter/Photo Reconnaissance Squadron
HT	Helicopter Training Squadron	VMO	Marine Observation Squadron
HU	Helicopter Utility Squadron	VMGR	Marine Air Refueling/Transport Squadron
VA	Attack Squadron	VP	Patrol Squadron
VAK	Aerial Refueling Squadron	VPU	Patrol Squadron Special Operations
VAQ	Tactical Electronic Warfare Squadron	VQ	Fleet Air Reconnaissance Squadron
VAW	Carrier Airborne Early Warning Squadron	VR	Fleet Logistics Squadron
		VRF	Air Ferry Squadron
VC	Fleet Composition Squadron	VS	Antisubmarine Squadron
		VT	Training Squadron
		VX	Air Test and Evaluation Squadron
		VXE	Antarctic Development Squadron
		VXN	Oceanic Development Squadron

rcraft by the letter 'V'. It has been assumed that the 'Z' was used in deference to the great Count von Zeppelin, an early proponent of the airship. But this cannot be verified. Also, no conclusive evidence has been found as to why the letter 'V' was chosen for heavier-than-air aircraft. The French words *vol plané,* meaning 'gliding flight', are generally assumed to be the answer, but this cannot be proven. The current prefixes are shown in the box above.

Launching and Landing Aircraft on an Aircraft Carrier.

The launch and recovery of aircraft on a carrier is a very complex, fast and highly dangerous activity. The four deck-edge elevators on the US carriers each have the capacity to carry two aircraft to and from the four and a half acre hangar deck of a *Nimitz*-class aircraft carrier within seconds. The aircraft must then be marshalled very precisely on the carrier's flight-deck to allow them to be launched quickly and in the proper sequence, and without causing a 'traffic-jam' when moving them around the deck to and from the catapults or the arrester wires.

Each carrier has four powerful steam-driven catapults, two on the bow and two at the waist on the angled flight-deck. Each is capable of launching an aircraft weighing up to 30 tons. When the aircraft is ready and positioned for a launch the catapult's shuttle is locked on to the aircraft's nose gear. From a standing start, and with the aircraft engines at full power and the after-burners alight, on release the shuttle will pull the aircraft down the flight-deck to a take-off speed of 165 mph in two seconds flat, all within 300 feet, launching the aircraft into the air over the end of the carrier's flight-deck. During the daylight hours the carrier has the capability to launch two aircraft every 37 seconds at the same time as one lands. At night the launch and landing rate is reduced to one of each per minute.

Angling a 'landing deck' out from the main 'take-off strip' (see pages 21, 32 and 33) gives the carrier the ability to simultaneously launch and recover aircraft. It provides the aircraft that are about to land a clear deck ahead, free from the parked aircraft that would normally occupy the flight-deck. The jets are travelling at 150 mph, just above their stalling speed, when making their landing approach. The pilot is aided by the Landing Signals Officers (LSOs), who help by talking him or her in, and the carrier's primary visual glideslope indicator, the Fresnal Lense (see page 43), which is positioned on the port side of the carrier. As the aircraft touches its wheels on to the deck the pilot increases the engine power so that if he or she misses the arrester wires (the 'trap') the aircraft will have enough power to take to the air again ('bolting') and fly round to make another landing attempt.

Many people who have experienced a carrier landing have referred to it as basically a 'controlled crash'. Fixed-wing aircraft have a tailhook on the end of an eight-foot bar under the rear of the plane which can be lowered and extended from the stern of the aircraft. The tailhook is fully extended on the approach to the carrier, and on hitting the deck it catches on one of the four steel arrester wires which are stretched across the flight-deck. This brings the aircraft to a complete stop within just 320 feet – always at the same place regardless of the aircraft's size or weight. There are four wires numbered from the stern; the pilot will always aim to catch number three. Landings are carefully monitored by the Landing Signals Officers, who are themselves experienced aviators. They stand on the side of the deck assessing the aircraft as it approaches the landing, helping the pilot over the radio. Each pilot will be judged and given grades by the LSO according to how good the landing was, and will be criticised accordingly.

Once safely down and after raising the hook and dropping the wire, which is then re-spooled ready for the next landing, the aircraft must quickly taxi away from the landing area and park, making room for any following aircraft to land.

Helicopter Landing

Helicopters are challenging enough to fl never mind trying to land one on to a sma pitching flight-deck on the stern of a shi such as a frigate, in the middle of a storn night at sea.

Usually the helicopter approaches th ship's stern on a 30º to 40º angle to its cours therefore avoiding the air turbulan generated by the ship's superstructure, whic can be considerable when the ship travelling at speed into a strong headwin The helicopter will then position itself ov the frigate's flight-deck, lining up with painted stripe and with its nose above positioning mark. On receiving the signal th it is safe to land, the pilot has to judge whe the motion of the ship is relatively stable f him or her to then lose altitude and, with fu downward pitch on the rotor blades, plant t landing gear safely on the frigate's fligh deck. On touchdown the flight-deck crew w then quickly use tie-down chains and choc to secure the helicopter to the deck.

In extreme weather conditions, where i amount of pilot skills will help, the RA (Recovery Assist, Secure and Traverse) syste is used. A light, or 'messenger', cable lowered to the frigates flight-deck and connected to the main 'haul-down' cab which is then hauled up to the helicopter ar automatically locked into the main RA probe. At the appropriate moment the L applies tension to the haul-down cable, whi produces a stabilising effect to the hover, ar the aircraft is pulled down to the corre landing spot on the frigate's-flight deck.

The number of aircraft operated by the l Navy and Marine Corps has been mu reduced over the last decade or so, b between them they still possess the secor most potent airforce in the world, second on to the USAF. The acknowledged superb lev of training that the fleet pilots receive and t excellent aircraft they fly make for a Navy ar Marine Corps which are more than a mat for any other airforce in the world. T following pages give photographic covera of these aircraft, along with views from t flight-deck.

ver the western
cific in October
003, four F/A-18E
per Hornets
ssigned to Strike
ghter Squadron Four
ne (VFA-41) – the
lack Aces' – in a
ack formation. They
re from Carrier Air
ing Eleven (CVW-11),
om the USS *Nimitz*
arrier Strike Group.
he Super Hornet is a
ghly capable muti-
le warplane. Its roles
e air superiority,
ghter escort, armed
connaissance, aerial
-flight refuelling,
ose air support, air-
efence suppression,
d day/night
nventional and
recision strike using
ser-, infrared- and
PS-guided weapons.
hen compared with
e F-14 Tomcat,
hich it will
ventually replace, the
per Hornet has 40%
wer costs per flight
ur and requires 75%
ss maintenance
urs per flight hours.
e F/A-18E/F has a
nger range than the
rlier A to D models
d will eventually
place all of them. It
4 ft 4 in. longer, 100
. ft larger in area,
d has a 40% increase
range over the F/A-
3C/D. The Super
ornet's first
perational cruise
gan aboard the
rrier USS *Abraham
ncoln,* in July 2002,
here the aircraft saw
s first combat on
ovember 6, 2002,
ccessfully striking
ostile targets in Iraq.

Above: An F/A-18C Hornet of Strike Fighter Squadron Three Seven (VFA-37) – the 'Bulls' – which was embarked aboard the USS *Harry S. Truman* (CVN 75), flying over northern Iraq in April 2003. The USS *Harry S. Truman* and her Carrier Air Wing Three (CVW-3) were conducting combat missions in support of Operation Iraqi Freedom.

Below: An F-14 of Fighter Squadron Three Two (VF-32) – the 'Swordsmen' – over northern Iraq in April 2003. VF-32 was also embarked aboard the USS *Harry S. Truman*. The F-14 Tomcat is a mach-2, twin-engine, variable-sweep-wing fighter whose primary roles are air superiority, fleet air defence and precision strike against ground targets.

Above: A four-'ship' formation of F/A-18 Hornets of the US Navy 'Blue Angels' aerobatic team performing at the 2002 'Awlins' Air Show at New Orleans. The Blue Angels were formed in 1946 and have flown various aircraft over the years. The team is composed of six planes, five being flown by Navy pilots and one by a Marine Corps pilot.

Below: Over the Arabian Gulf on November 30, 2003, an EA-6B Prowler of Electronic Attack Squadron One Three Seven (VAQ-137) – the 'Rooks' – flies a mission in support of Operation Iraqi Freedom. VAQ-137 was deployed with Carrier Air Wing One (CVW-1) aboard the USS *Enterprise* (CVN 65) at the time.

Above: Aboard the USS *Essex* (LHD 2), a helicopter/dock-landing ship, an Aviation Boatswain's Mate gives the go-ahead for an AV-8B Harrier attack plane to land vertically on to the ship's flight-deck. The USS *Essex* had embarked the 31st Marine Expeditionary Unit (MEU) and was participating in Exercise Tandem Thrust 2003. This was a joint military exercise of forces from the United States, Canada and Australia, held in the Northern Mariana Islands in the Philippine Sea, April 2003.

Below: A Northrop Grumman E-2C Hawkeye (lower) in company with a C-2A Greyhound. The Hawkeye has a large rotodome perched on the top of the fuselage for its airborne early warning radar. The Greyhound is a specially designed derivative of the Hawkeye and is a shipboard transport aircraft.

Above: A P-3C Orion Maritime Patrol aircraft assigned to Patrol Squadron Eight (VP-8) – the 'Tigers' – flies along the coastline of Sicily on May 26, 2003. VP-8 is home-based in Brunswick, Maine, and was deployed to Naval Air Station (NAS) Sigonella, Sicily, to provide support to the US Sixth Fleet and NATO forces in the Mediterranean Sea.

Below: An S-3B Viking of Sea Control Squadron Two Nine (VS-29) – the 'Dragonfires' – of Carrier Air Wing Eleven (CVW-11) from the USS *Nimitz* Carrier Strike Group in the western Pacific Ocean, October 2003. The Viking is a carrier-borne ASW (anti-submarine warfare) and tanker aircraft. The internal weapons bay can house four torpedoes, sonabuoys, mines, depth charges or bombs, plus two underwing hardpoints that can each carry a torpedo or Harpoon or Maverick missile. The Viking can also carry underwing buddy tanker pods for in-flight refuelling of other aircraft.

Above: A T-45C Goshawk of Training Squadron Seven (VT- – the 'Eagles' – on th flight-deck of the US *Harry S. Truman* (CV 75), July 2003. The Goshawk is a variant of the British designe Hawk trainer aircraf which has been modified and built under licence in the USA.

Left: A CH-53E Super Stallion of Marine Medium Helicopter Squadron One Six Three (HMM-163) – t 'Ridge Runners' – lift off from the flight-deck of USS *Peleliu* (LHA 5) in the Arabia Sea. The Super Stalli is a three-engined, a greatly improved, development of the Sea Stallion.

Above: A Sea King UH-3 Search and Rescue helicopter takes off from Naval Station Everett, Washington, during an exercise. Once the Sea King formed the backbone of the US Navy's ASW helicopter force, but it has been largely replaced by the SH-60 Seahawk.

Right: A CH-46 Sea Knight of Helicopter Combat Support Squadron One One (HC-11) – the 'Gunbearers' – transfers cargo from the USS Bridge (AOE-10) to the USS Nimitz (CVN 68) in a connected replenishment operation (CONREP) during Operation Iraqi Freedom.

Above: Two HH-60H Seahawk helicopters from the Helicopter Anti-Submarine Squadron One One (HS-11) – the 'Dragon Slayers' – lifting off from the flight-deck of the USS *Shreveport* (LPD 12) in December 2001. The stub wings on the side of the fuselage can carry various offensive weapons, including torpedoes, depth charges and air-to-surface missiles, such as the AGM-114 Hellfire missiles, as seen here.

Below: AH-1W Super Cobra attack helicopters from Marine Light Attack Helicopter Squadron Two Six Nine (HMLA-269) aboard the USS *Saipan* (LHA 2) prior to lift off, January 2003. The Super Cobra is armed with a nose-mounted three-barrel 20-mm cannon, and has the ability to carry rocket pods and as many as eight TOW or Hellfire anti-armour missiles, two machine-gun pods or two Sidewinder air-to-air missiles.

Above: In the Arabian Gulf, April 2003, an F/A-18E Super Hornet is moved manually on the flight-deck of the USS *Abraham Lincoln* (CVN 72). The USS *Abraham Lincoln,* and her Carrier Air Wing Fourteen (CVW-14), were conducting combat operations during Operation Iraqi Freedom.

Below: An F/A-18E Super Hornet from Strike Fighter Squadron Four One (VFA-41) – the 'Black Aces' – of Carrier Air Wing Eleven (CVW-11), from the USS *Nimitz* Carrier Strike Group, while on deployment in the western Pacific in October 2003.

Above: An F/A-18C Hornet of Strike Fighter Squadron Eight Six (VFA-86) – the 'Sidewinders' – about to be launched from the flight-deck of the USS *Enterprise* (CVN 65), Arabian Gulf, December 2003. The steam is from the catapult track and has been generated by the previous launch.

Below: The catapult officer, or 'Shooter', gives the signal for a two-seater F/A-18D Hornet of Strike Fighter Squadron One Zero Six (VFA-106) – the 'Gladiators' – to launch from the flight-deck of USS *Theodore Roosevelt*. The Hornet has a maximum speed of mach 1.8, approximately 1,200 mph, and a maximum combat range of over 1,000 miles.

Above: A two-seater F/A-18F Super Hornet from Strike Fighter Squadron One Two Two (VFA-122) – the 'Flying Eagles' – launches from one of the two steam-powered catapults on the bow of the USS *John C. Stennis* (CVN 74), December 2003. The carrier was conducting training exercises off the southern California coast.

Below: An F/A-18C Hornet takes on fuel from an F/A-18D Super Hornet during in-flight refuelling training. One of the subsidiary roles the Super Hornet has to perform is that of an in-flight tanker, since the retirement of the Grumman KA-6D Intruder tanker back in 1996. This role is also performed by the Lockheed Martin S-3B Viking.

Above: A pilot of Strike Fighter Squadron One One Three (VFA-113) – the 'Stingers' – entering Iraqi airspace in an F/A-18C Hornet during Operation Iraqi Freedom. The Stingers were embarked aboard USS *Abraham Lincoln* (CVN 72) with Carrier Air Wing Fourteen (CVW-14), and were conducting combat operations as part of Operation Iraqi Freedom. The pilot's Hornet and that of his companion are both armed with free-fall bombs, laser-guided bombs, and Sidewinder missiles, plus their 20-mm cannon.

Below: An F/A-18 Hornet of Strike Fighter Squadron Eight Two (VFA-82) – the 'Marauders' – during Operation Enduring Freedom in November 2003. VFA-82 was with Carrier Air Wing One (CVW-1) aboard USS *Enterprise* (CVN 65) in the north Arabian Sea. Note the JDAM GPS-guided bomb and Sidewinder on the port wing, and laser-guided bomb and fuel tank on the starboard wing.

Above: The view a pilot sees as he or she approaches the USS *George Washington* (CVN 73) during the final approach for an arrested landing (nicknamed the 'trap'). The four arrester wires can just be made out stretched across the flight-deck. The photograph was taken in November 2002 when the USS *George Washington* and her Carrier Air Wing Seventeen (CVW-17) were on a six-month deployment supporting Operations Enduring Freedom and Southern Watch.

Below: An F/A-18C Hornet of Marine Fighter Attack Training Squadron One Zero One – the 'Sharpshooters' – with tail hook extended, is about to touch down on the deck of the USS *Theodore Roosevelt* (CVN 71), November 2003. The nuclear-powered aircraft carrier was conducting carrier qualifications in the Atlantic Ocean.

Four F-14 Tomcats from Fighter Squadron Three One (VF-31) – the 'Tomcatters'. VF-31 was with Carrier Air Wing Fourteen (CVW-14) embarked on the USS *John Stennis* at the time the photograph was taken, November 2003. There have been three variants of the F-14 Tomcat to enter full service with the US Navy, the F-14A, F-14B and the F-14D. The F-14B and D models have more powerful engines the F-14A.

ght: An F-14D Tomcat of
ghter Squadron Two Three
ne (VF-231) – the 'Black
ons' – from Carrier Air Wing
ght (CVW-8) aboard the USS
heodore Roosevelt during
peration Iraqi Freedom. Note
e twin IRST/TV (infra-red
arch/track sensor and TV
mera) pods under the nose.
nly 37 F-14Ds have been
ilt, plus 18 F-14As rebuilt
 F-14Ds. The Tomcat has a
p speed of over mach 2 and
service ceiling of 50,000
et. It can carry a mix of
oenix, Sparrow and
dewinder missiles or a mix
 dumb and precision-guided
ombs, as well as its
ternally mounted Vulcan
-mm cannon.

low: An F-14 Tomcat from
ghter Squadron Two One One
F-211) – the 'Checkmates' –
unches from the flight-deck
 the USS *Enterprise* (CVN 65),
ptember 2003. The Tomcat
 capable of carrying 14,500 lb
 expendable weapons and
uipment.

Above: An F-14D Tomcat of Fighter Squadron Two (VF-2) – the 'Bounty Hunters' – climbs away from its carrier, the USS *Constellation* (CV 64), on May 13, 2003. Note that the plane's tail hook is extended. The *Constellation* and Carrier Air Wing Tw (CVW-2) were returning home after their deployment supporting Operations Enduring Freedom and Iraqi Freedom.

Below: An F-14 Tomcat from Fighter Squadron One Four Three (VF-143) – the 'Pukin' Dogs' – receiving its final maintenance checks, on the flight-deck of the USS *George Washington* (CVN 73), before an evening flight operation. Tomcat squadrons are gradually converting to F/A-18 E/F Super Hornets and this programme should be completed by 2007. The Tomcat will have been in US Navy service since 1972 – 35 years, a commendable record.

Right: An EA-6B Prowler from Electronic Attack Squadron One Three Seven (VAQ-137) – the 'Rooks' – flies a mission in support of Operation Iraqi Freedom, November 2003. VAQ-137 was deployed with Carrier Air Wing One (CVW-1) from the USS *Enterprise* (CVN 65).

Below: The EA-6B Prowler provides all-weather protection to strike aircraft, with the aid of advanced electronic counter-measures. It is a twin-engine aircraft with a four-man crew. As well as its ability to disrupt enemy electronic protection equipment, it is able to attack with HARM anti-radar missiles.

eft: An Aviation Boatswain's Mate prepares an EA-6B Prowler for launch from the USS *Theodore Roosevelt* (CVN 71). The rowler is powered by two Pratt & Whitney J52-P408 engines with 11,200 lb of thrust and a top speed of 575 mph. Its randard take-off weight is 55,000 lb and it can be armed with up to six AGM-88 HARM anti-radar missiles.

bove: A EA-6B Prowler of Electronic Attack Squadron One Forty One (VAQ-141) – the 'Shadow Hawks' – makes a 'touch-and- ʹ on the flight-deck of USS *Theodore Roosevelt* (CVN-71). The AE-6B combat systems include the ALQ-99 on-board receiver, ʹe ALQ-99 pod-mounted jamming system, the USQ-113 communications jamming system and HARM missile.

elow: An EA-6B Prowler of Electronic Attack Squadron One Thirty Five (VAQ-135) – the 'Black Ravens' – from Carrier Air ʹing Eleven (CVW-11) operating from USS *Nimitz* (CVN 68) in the western Pacific. The primary role of the Prowler is the uppression of enemy air defences by interrupting electronic activity and at the same time obtaining tactical electronic ʹtelligence.

Left: The X-35 (F-35 in service) comes in two variants, one with conventional take-off and landing and the other with STOVL (Short Take-Off and Vertical Landing). The STOVL variant is for service with the Marine Corps. The aircraft resembles a single-engined, scaled down F-22. The STOVL version also has a lift fan situated behind the cockpit.

Below: The stealthy, multi-role F-35 is intended to replace USAF F-16s, USN F/A-18s, and the Marine Corps' AV-8s. The carrier-capable model will have a larger area wing and tail and will be structurally strengthened for carrier operations.

Right: Aboard the USS *Bataan* (LHD 5) an AV-8 Harrier pilot gets a 'fuel update' from deck crew before taking off on a sortie during Operation Iraqi Freedom. The Marine Corps are the only US operators of this unique warplane, with its short take-off and vertical-landing capabilities (STOVL).

Below: The first Harriers were designed and flew in Great Britain in the 1960s. The aircraft has been updated and extensively improved, and the AV-8B is a larger, longer-range and generally more powerful aircraft than the earlier models. The AV-8B has a maximum external stores load of 13,000 lb, including precision-guided bombs, dumb bombs, Maverick and Sidewinder missiles, sensor pods, and an internally mounted 25-mm GAU-12 Gatling gun.

Left: An AV-8B Harrier approaching the flight-deck of the amphibious-assault ship US Peleliu (LHA 5) as it is about to land. The ship and her aircraft were part of Expeditionary Strike Group One (ESG-1) in the Arabian Sea, October 2003.

Below: An AV-8B Harrier performs a vertical take-off from the amphibious-assault ship US Tarawa (LHA 1). Tarawa was deployed in support of Operation Enduring Freedom in the Arabian Gulf, March 2003. The AV-8B Harrier has a top speed over 625 mph and a maximum service ceiling of 50,000 feet. It first entered service with the US Marine Corps in 1984; they ordered 280.

bove: A Northrop Grumman E-2C Hawkeye of Carrier Airborne Early Warning Squadron One Two Three (VAW-123) – the 'Screw ops' – from the USS *Enterprise* (CVN 65) in the Atlantic Ocean, September 2003. One hundred and thirty-nine Hawkeye aircraft ave entered US Navy service, the first model taking to the air in 1960. The plane has been successively upgraded over the years the current E-2C.

elow: The E-2C Hawkeye patrols at an altitude of 30,000 feet and is able to detect and assess targets at a range of over 300 iles. The radar rotodome attached to the upper fuselage is 24 feet in diameter. Its APS-145 radar is able to resist jamming, very capable in detecting targets over land as well as sea, and possesses the ability to track as many as 2,000 different rgets at the same time.

Right: The USS *Harry S. Truman* (CVN 75) in December 2002, with elements of Carrier Air Wing Three (CVW-3) shown on her flight-deck. The *Truman* was operating at the time within the Sixth Fleet's area of responsibility while in support of Operation Enduring Freedom. On deck can be seen 29 F/A-18 Hornets, eight F-14 Tomcats, two EA-6B Prowlers, three E-2C Hawkeyes, six S-3B Vikings and three Seahawk helicopters.

Below: Landing Signals Officers guide an E-2C Hawkeye of Squadron One One Three (VAW-113) – the 'Black Eagles' – on to the flight-deck of the USS *John C. Stennis* (CVN 74). The Hawkeye has a crew of five, the pilot, co-pilot, combat-information-centre officer, air-control officer and radar operator.

Opposite page, below: The E-2C Hawkeye has a maximum speed of 380 mph with a cruising speed of 300 mph and a service ceiling of 37,000 feet. It can spend four and a half hours on station while it is 200 miles from its carrier, seeking and identifying any enemy activity. Here an E-2C Hawkeye of One Two Four Carrier Airborne Early Warning Squadron (VAW-124) – the 'Bear Aces' – lands on the flight-deck of the USS *Theodore Roosevelt* (CVN 71) while in the Mediterranean Sea, April 2003. The carrier was there in support of Operation Iraqi Freedom.

Left: A formation of T-45A Goshawks of Training Squadron Two Two (VS-22) – the 'Golden Eagles' – flying from Naval Air Station (NAS) Kingsville, South Texas, October 2003. The Goshawk, an advanced carrier-capable trainer, is a replacement for both the TA-4J Skyhawk and the T-2 Buckeye, and first entered service in January 1992.

Below: The T-45A Goshawk has a maximum speed of 620 mph and a service ceiling of 40,000 feet; its maximum take-off weight is 14,000 lb. The US Navy plans to acquire a total of 234 aircraft, and in 2004 the current plan is to upgrade the T-45A models to T-45Cs.

Above: A T-45C Goshawk of Training Squadron Seven (VT-7) makes an FCLP (Field Carrier Landing Practice) aboard the USS *Harry S. Truman* (CVN 75) off the east coast of the United States, July 2003. The Goshawk has two hardpoints, one under each wing, which can carry practice bombs, rocket pods and fuel tanks.

Below: The last time the T-2C Buckeye was to be used to train student pilots aboard aircraft carriers. The T-2C Buckeye from Fixed Wing Training Squadron Nine (VT-9) performed a touch-and-go on the flight-deck of the USS *Harry S. Truman* (CVN 75) on July 16, 2003. Some 550 Buckeyes were built, the first entering service in 1959 and the last in 1977.

Above: The flight deck 'Shooter' looks to the centre-deck operator for the status of the steam pressure levels for the catapult prior to launching an S-3B Viking of Sea Control Squadron Three Three (VS-33) – the 'Screwbirds'. The Viking has a crew of four – two pilots, a tactical coordinator and a sensor operator – and has been in service since 1974. In April 2004, VS-29 – the 'Dragonfires' – and VS-38 – the 'Red Griffins' – were disestablished as the Viking began to be slowly retired from US Navy service. The final squadron chosen for disestablishment, VS-22 – the 'Checkmates' – is scheduled to be disbanded in January 2009.

Below: An S-3B Viking of Sea Control Squadron Three Five (VS-35) – the 'Blue Wolves' – folds its wings after making an arrested landing on the USS *John C. Stennis* (CVN 74). VS-35 was part of Carrier Air Wing Fourteen (CVW-14) aboard the USS *John C. Sten* which was training in the Pacific Ocean, November 2003. The well-armed Viking, while on an anti-submarine-warfare patrol, maintains a speed of 185 mph, giving it an operational radius of over 1,000 miles and an endurance of seven and a half hours.

above: The Viking's other role is that of the US Navy's carrier-based in-flight tanker plane. Seen here is an S-3B Viking of Sea Control Squadron Two Four (VS-24) – the 'Scouts' – refuelling an EA-6B Prowler of Electronic Attack Squadron One Four One (VAQ-141) – the 'Shadow Hawks' – of Carrier Air Wing Eight (CVW-8) from the USS *Theodore Roosevelt* (CVN 71).

below: A P-3 Orion of Patrol Squadron Three Zero (VP-30) – the 'Pros Nest' – flying with bomb-bay doors open. This land-based Navy maritime patrol aircraft has been in service since 1962. The current version, the P-3C, was introduced in 1969. Its internal weapons bay can accommodate eight anti-submarine torpedoes or eight depth bombs.

Left: This P-3C Orion aircraft is carrying two AIM-9 Sidewinder short-range air-to-air missiles on its outboard wing pylons and four AGM-84 Harpoon anti-ship missiles under the wings and fuselage. The Harpoon is an all-weather, over-the-horizon, anti-ship missile system adapted for use with P-3 aircraft in 1979.

Above: A P-3C Orion aircraft of Patrol Squadron Eight (VP-8) – the 'Tigers' – flies over Mt Etna in Italy. VP-8 was providing logistical support for the US Sixth Fleet and NATO forces in the Mediterranean Sea, May 2003. The Orion has a maximum speed of 470 mph and a cruising speed of 375 mph. Its mission radius is 1,500 miles and it has a maximum endurance of seventeen hours.

Right: A tactical coordinator (TACCO) station of a P-3C Orion aircraft of Patrol Squadron Nine (VP-9) – the 'Golden Eagles'. The Orion has a crew of ten, comprising of two pilots, flight engineer, navigator, tactical coordinator, two acoustic-sensor operators, a Magnetic Anomaly Detector (MAD), and two observers/sonabouy loaders.

Above: A Marine Corps KC-130 Hercules refuels a CH-53E Sea Stallion helicopter from the 31st Marine Expeditionary Unit (31st MEU) during a long-range personnel-recovery training mission. The KC-130 Hercules is the primary Marine Corps tanker for aerial refuelling squadrons. It is the world's most successful and prolific postwar aircraft, first flying in 1954.

Below: A Marine Corps KC-130 Hercules of Aerial Refueler/Transport Squadron Three Five Two (VMGR-352) – the 'Raiders' – prepares for a mission at a forward operating base during Operation Enduring Freedom in Afghanistan, Febuary 2002. Another KC-130 is taking off as it begins a transport mission, flying back to Kandahar Airport. The KC-130's standard seating layout is for 92 fully equipped troops or 64 paratroops, or 72 stretcher patients plus two medical attendants. It is also capable of transporting light-armoured vehicles and artillery. The Hercules has a maximum cruising speed of 370 mph and a range (with a 20,000-lb payload) of 4,700 miles. Its range with a maximum payload of 45,000 lb is 2,420 miles.

\bove: A C-2 Greyhound of Carrier Logistic Support Squadron Four Zero (VRC-40) – the 'Rawhides' – makes an arrested \nding on the flight-deck of the USS *Harry S. Truman* (CVN 75). The C-2A Greyhound is an adaptation of the E-2 Hawkeye, \th a broader fuselage, upturned tail and rear-loading cargo door. It can fly at up to 350 mph and has a service ceiling of \,500 feet. The Greyhound provides a vital transport link between carriers at sea and shore bases.

\low: A 'Shooter' signals a C-2A Greyhound of Fleet Logistics Support Squadron Four Zero (VRC-40) to launch from the \ght-deck of the USS *Theodore Roosevelt* (CVN 71), November 2003. The Greyhound has a maximum payload of 10,000 lb, ` 39 passengers/20 stretcher patients plus medical staff. It was first flown in 1964 and the initial batch of 17 planes \tered service in 1966, another eight joined them in 1970–1, and 39 more were ordered in 1982, entering service between \86 and 1989.

Above: An F-14A Tomcat of Fighter Squadron Two One One (VF-211) – the 'Checkmates' – launches from the flight-deck of th
USS *Enterprise* (CVN 65) as two F/A-18C Hornets await their turn to launch, Arabian Gulf, November 2003. Note the size of je
blast deflectors (JBDs) that separate the two Hornets.

Below: Aviation Boatswain's Mates change arresting-wire springs on the flight-deck of the USS *John C. Stennis* (CVN 74). The
springs raise the arresting wire above the flight-deck, allowing the tail hook of the aircraft that is landing to catch it.

Right: The Datum Lights of the Improved Fresnal Lens Optical Landing System (FLOLS) – nicknamed the 'Meatball' – aboard the USS *George Washington* (CVN 73). The Fresnal Lens is the primary visual glideslope indicator for the carrier and is located on the port side of the flight-deck. It aids pilots to adjust visually for a good glide path during the final approach to the carrier.

Right: The Landing Signals Officer (LSO) monitoring an F/A-18C Hornet of Strike Fighter Squadron Eight Seven (VFA-87) – the 'War Party' – as it comes in to land on the flight-deck of the USS *Theodore Roosevelt* (CVN 71), January 2003. VFA-87 was part of Carrier Air Wing Eight (CVW-8).

Right: An F/A-18 Hornet of Strike Fighter Squadron Nine Four (VFA-94) – the 'Mighty Shrikes' – at the moment it makes a 'trap', brought to a halt by one of the arrester wires aboard the USS *Nimitz* (CVN 68). The *Nimitz* and Carrier Air Wing Eleven (CVW-11) were in the Indian Ocean, April 2003, before joining the forces supporting Operation Iraqi Freedom.

Opposite page, top left: Aviation Ordnancemen conducting maintenance on a 20-mm Vulcan Cannon, as fitted on the F/A-18 and the F-14. This Gatling-type gun has a six-barrelled rotary action which is powered by the aircraft's hydraulic and electrical supply. The gun has a phenomenal rate of fire of 100 rounds a second.

Opposite page, top right: A Sidewinder air-to-air missile on the wing tip of an F/A-18. The Sidewinder homes in on the hot exhaust from its target's engines. It has a range of over 12 miles, a speed of mach 2.5, and has a warhead weighing over 20 lb.

Opposite page, bottom: A heavily armed F/A-18 Hornet equipped with eight AIM-120 AMRAAM (Advanced Medium-Range Air-to-Air missiles) under the wings, plus two attached to the aircraft's fuselage and two Sidewinders on the wing-tip rails. The AMRAAM has a radar seeker that allows it to track down its targets, a range of over 30 miles, and a warhead weighing 50 lb.

Above: An F-14 Tomcat of Fighter Squadron One Zero Three (VF-103) – the 'Jolly Rogers' – fires a Phoenix air-to-air missile. The Phoenix is the Navy's only long-range air-to-air missile. It has an airborne weapons control system with multiple-target handling capabilities. It is radar guided and has a range in excess of 100 miles and a warhead weighing over 130 lb.

Below: An Aviation Ordnanceman takes a moment to rest on an AIM-7 Sparrow during flight operations aboard the USS Abraham Lincoln (CVN 72). The AIM-7 Sparrow medium-range air-to-air missile is a Semi-Active Radar Homing (SARH) weapon. During the Gulf War of 1991, the Sparrow acquitted itself well, accounting for 25 of the 42 enemy planes shot down. Eventually it will be totally replaced by the AMRAAM.

Opposite page, top and bottom: Aviation Ordnancemen moving AGM-54 Joint Stand-off Weapons (JSOW) on to the flight-deck of the USS *Kitty Hawk* (CV 63), from one of the ship's weapons elevators during 'Iraqi Freedom', March 2003. The JSOW is an adverse-weather, short-range, stand-off anti-armour/SEAD (Suppression of Enemy Air Defenses) dispenser weapon. It is designed to deliver sub-munitions in much the same way as a cluster bomb does. The wings, seen here folded back, aid the weapon during the glide stage of an attack. It was first used in combat during Operation Allied Force in 1999 when USN F/A-18s used it to attack Serbian SAM radars. The JSOW is a 1,000-lb smart bomb that can be launched from distances up to 40 miles from its target. GPS technology is used for targeting. The weapon is referred to as Joint because it is used jointly by the US Air Force, US Navy and US Marine Corps.

Above: Aviation Ordnancemen move a JDAM GPS-guided bomb on the flight-deck of the USS *Abraham Lincoln* (CVN 72). The *Abraham Lincoln* and Carrier Air Wing Fourteen (CVW-14) were conducting combat operations supporting Operation Iraqi Freedom. This JDAM is a 2,000-lb Mk-84 'dumb' bomb that has been reconfigured by attaching a GPS guidance unit and fins which turn it into a precision-guided bomb, a GBU-31.

Below: Aboard the USS *Theodore Roosevelt* (CVN 71) during Operation Iraqi Freedom, with ordnance on the ship's flight-deck. Uppermost are two JSOWs, then two JDAMs, a dozen laser-guided bombs on their trolleys, and two dumb bombs.

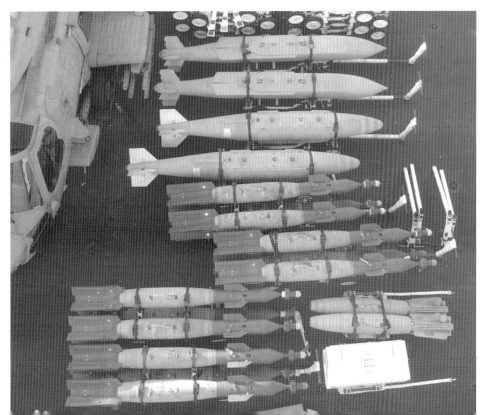

Left: Aviation Ordnancemen inspect an Mk-63 Quick Strike Mine prior to it being loaded on t an F/A-18C Hornet aboard the US *John C. Stennis* (CVN 74).

Right: During Operation Iraqi Freedom, March 2003, a female deck-crew airman of the 'Gauntlets', Electronic Attack Squadron One Three Six (VAQ-136) of Carrier Air Wing Five (CVW-5), signals that an EA-6B Prowler aircraft is ready on the USS *Kitty Hawk* (CV 63). The missile seen on the EA-6B Prowle is a high-speed anti-radiation missile (HARM) specifically designed for attacking radar sites

Below: F/A-18 Hornets loaded with dumb and precision-guided laser bombs stand ready on the flight-deck of the USS *Kitty Hawk* (CV 63) during Operation Iraqi Freedom.

Above: Patrol Squadron One Six (VP-16) using an electric bomb hoist to load an AGM-84D Harpoon missile on to a P-3 Orion. The Harpoon is a sea-skimming missile with a 490-lb warhead and a range of 60 miles. It is designed for knocking-out ships.

Below: Aviation Ordnancemen of Patrol Squadron Four Six (VP-46) – the 'Grey Knights' – loading an AGM-65 Maverick missile on to the wing of a P-3C Orion. VP-46 was deployed on missions in support of Operation Iraqi Freedom. The Maverick missile is 8 ft 2 in. long, with a wing span of 2 ft 4 in. The infra-red version weighs in at 485 lb and the TV version at 463 lb, and both can have either a shaped-charge or blast-fragmentation warhead.

ght: Aviation
rdnancemen secure a
and-off Land Attack
ssile-Expanded
esponse (SLAM-ER) to
a S-3B Viking of Sea
ontrol Squadron
aree One (VS-31) – the
op Cats' – aboard the
SS *George Washington*
VN 73). The SLAM-ER
an evolutionary
pgrade to the combat-
roven SLAM
ay/night, adverse-
reather over-the-
prizon, precision-
rike missile. The
.AM-ER is used
tclusively by US Navy
quadrons. It evolved
om the AGM-84E
and-off Land Attack
ssile (SLAM) which
ad itself evolved from
ae AGM-84 sea-
cimming Harpoon
ssile. This was done
y replacing the
arpoon's seeker head
ith an Imaging Infra-
ed (IIR) seeker as used
y the AGM-65D
averick, plus a GPS
ceiver and a datalink
r targeting.

ight: Inspecting
rdnance on an
H-1W Super Cobra
efore flight operations
om the amphibious-
ssault ship the USS
aipan (LHA 2) during
peration Iraqi
eedom, March 2003.
our AGM-114 Hellfire
ser-guided anti-tank
issiles as well as a
AU-68 70-mm rocket
od can be seen on the
elicopter's stub wing.
ae Hellfire has a
eadly 14-lb shaped-
aarge warhead. During
peration Desert
orm, in 1991,
ellfires knocked out
ver 500 Iraqi tanks.

The amphibious-assault ship USS *Kearsarge* (LHD 3) conducting combat missions in support of Operation Iraqi Freedom i
March 2003. The deck is loaded with CH-53E Super Stallion helicopters of Marine Heavy Helicopter Squadron Four Six Fou
(HMH-464) – the 'Condors'. In the assault mode the *Kearsarge* is capable of operating 6 AV-8B Harriers and 32 CH-46 Sea
Knight (or fewer CH-53 Super Stallion) helicopters. Or in the carrier mode, 20 AV-8B Harriers and 6 SH-60B Seahawk ASW
helicopters.

Above: Marines from 1st Marine Air Wing off-loading a UH-1 Huey helicopter from a transport ship. The Huey first flew in 1956 and has a special place in modern aviation history as it has been built in greater numbers, over 9,000, than any other western aircraft since World War Two. Over the years it has been gradually replaced by more modern types, but the few that are still in service are seen as useful aircraft for utility and transport duties.

Below: An HH-1M Huey Search and Rescue (SAR) helicopter at Naval Station Guantanamo Bay, Cuba, December 2003. The Huey has a maximum speed of 135 mph and a range in the region of 350 miles. It is still in service with nearly 40 countries.

Above: The Marine Corps AH-1 Super Cobra has proved itself to be a truly effective combat helicopter, able to carry a wide range of weaponry, including TOW (Tube-launched, Opitically tracked, Wire-Guided) anti-tank missiles, Hellfire laser-guided anti-tank missiles, unguided rocket pods, as well as possessing a three-barrelled 20-mm cannon. It is also able to carry Sidewinder air-to-air missiles. It is powered by two 1,723-shp turbo-shaft engines, and has a top speed of 219 mph and a range of 395 miles. Its empty weight is 10,200 lb, with a maximum take-off weight of 14,750 lb.

Below: An AH-1 Super Cobra of Helicopter Light Attack Squadron Three Six Seven (HMLA-367) fires a salvo of 70-mm rockets from rocket pods attached to its stub wings during a training mission. HMLA-367 is attached to the 1st Marine Air Wing (MAW

n Aviation Boatswain's Mate signals to an AH-1W Super Cobra helicopter of the Marine Air Group 29 embarked aboard the
nphibious-assault ship USS *Saipan* (LHA-2) in January 2003. The 20-mm M197 three-barrelled rotary cannon can be seen in
e helicopter's chin turret. The cannon has a nominal rate of fire of 750 rounds per minute. The AH-1W pilot sits in the rear
ockpit and the co-pilot/gunner in the front. In the nose is the high-resolution FLIR (Forward-Looking Infrared) dual-field-of-
view low-light television camera and laser rangefinder designator.

Above: An AH-1W Super Cobra from the 'Gunrunner' Marine Helicopter Attack Light Squadron Two Six Nir (HMA/L-269), aboard the US *Kearsarge* (LHD 3). The Sup Cobra is armed with Hellfir laser-guided anti-tank missiles and pods for free-flight 70-mm air-to-ground rockets. The Hellfire has a maximum range of five miles.

Left: An AH-1W Super Cobr of Marine Helicopter Mediu Squadron One Six Five (HMI 165), with the 13th Marine Expeditionary Unit (MEU) Special Operations Capable (SOC) Aviation Combat Element, takes off from the flight-deck of USS *Bonhomr Richard* (LHD 6) during March 2002. It is armed wit Hellfire laser-guided anti-tank missiles and pods for free-flight 70-mm air-to-ground rockets.

Above: Two HH-60H Seahawks of Helicopter Anti-Submarine Squadron One One (HS-11) – the 'Dragonslayers' – fly alongside the *Ticonderoga*-class guided-missile cruiser USS *Vella Gulf* (CG 72). The Seahawk has an empty weight of 13,500 lb and a maximum take-off weight of 22,000 lb. It was first deployed in 1991. It is powered by two 1,900-shp engines giving it a top speed of 170 mph and a combat radius of 150 nautical miles on a four-hour mission.

Right: An SH-60B from the guided-missile frigate USS *McInerney* (FFG 8) conducts a vertical replenishment with the destroyer USS *Stump* (DD 978). The SH-60B is intended for use aboard US Navy cruisers, destroyers and frigates as part of these warships' anti-submarine suites. It is able to carry anti-submarine torpedoes, sonobuoys and a towed Magnetic Anomaly Detector (MAD), which can be seen attached to the starboard stores pylon.

Above: Maintenance of an SH-60B Seahawk of Light Helicopter Anti-Submarine Squadron Four Four (HSL-44) – the 'Swamp Foxes' – aboard the guided-missile cruiser USS *Cape St George* (CG 71) in the Mediterranean Sea, March 2003, during Operation Iraqi Freedom. Note the tail in the folded position for ease of storage in the ships hangar.

Below: An SH-60 Seahawk of Light Helicopter Anti-Submarine Squadron Four Two (HSL-42) – the 'Proud Warriors' – after lifting off from the flight-deck of the guided-missile frigate USS *Boone* (FFG 28), February 2003.

above: An SH-60B Seahawk from Helicopter Anti-Submarine Light Five One (HSL-51) fires an AGM-119 Penguin anti-ship missile, July 2002. The Penguin is a highly effective Norwegian-designed missile which is in service with the US Navy. It has a launch weight of 840 lb and a range of 22-plus miles; the semi-armour-piercing warhead weighs 250 lb.

below right: The view the Aviation Warfare Systems Operator has when scanning for surface contacts with the Forward Looking Infrared Pod (FLIR) on an SH-60F Seahawk.

Left: An SH-60 Seahawk transferring ammunition from the USS *Theodore Roosevelt* (CVN 71) to the USS *George Washington* (CVN 73) while the ships were underway in the Atlantic Ocean, November 2003. The Seahawk has a ventral cargo hook capable of lifting 6,000 lb.

Right: Aviation Warfare Systems Operator checking the tail-rotor gearbox of an SH-60F Seahawk on the flight-deck of the USS *Kitty Hawk* (CV 63). This is one of the many pre-flight checks that are carried out before operations.

Below: An HH-60H Seahawk of Helicopter Anti-Submarine Squadron Five (HS-5) – the 'Nightdippers' – about to land on the flight-deck of the guided-missile frigate USS *Elrod* (FFG 55). The HH-60H has a crew of four and is able to carry eight passengers.

pposite page, top: A CH-46 Sea Knight of Marine Helicopter Medium Squadron One Six Five (HMM-165) during Operation esert Storm in 1991. This helicopter is about to land aboard the battleship USS *Wisconsin* (BB 64). These twin-rotor elicopters still soldier on after being in service for over four decades. The current D/E models were introduced in 1978.

pposite page, bottom: A Navy CH-46 Sea Knight from Helicopter Combat Support Squadron Eight (HC-8) in June 2003. The H-46 will begin to be replaced with the MH-60S Knighthawk in the US Navy in the autumn of 2004. The Sea Knight is)wered by two 1,770 shp engines, giving it a top speed of 166 mph and a service ceiling of over 10,000 feet.

bove: A CH-46 Sea Knight, with an AH-1W Super Cobra in the background, lifts off from the flight-deck of USS *Peleliu* (LHA , in the Arabian Sea, October 2003. The CH-46 crew consists of four: the pilot, co-pilot, crew chief and mechanic.

elow: Two CH-46 Sea Knights and a UH-60 Blackhawk land on a road near the Jalibah airstrip in Iraq to take on additional el before continuing with their mission, flying northward to carry supplies and Marines forward during Operation Iraqi eedom in March 2003. The Sea Knight can carry a maximum of 22 troops plus two aerial gunners or a 5,000-lb payload.

Opposite page, top:
An Aviation
Boatswain's Mate
watches as a CH-46
Sea Knight lands on
the flight-deck of USS
John C. Stennis (CVN
74). The Sea Knight is
from Helicopter
Combat Support
Squadron One One
(HC-11) – the
'Gunbearers'. The
maximum take-off
weight of a CH-46 is
just over 24,000 lb. It
has a height of 16 ft 8
in., a length of 84 ft 4
in., and a width of 51
feet. These
measurements are
with the rotors spead.

**Opposite page,
bottom:** An SH-60
Seahawk and three
CH-46 Sea Knights
about to take off from
the flight-deck of USS
Wasp (LHD 1) while
the ship was on
exercise in the Gulf of
Mexico, December
2003. As well as being
able to carry troops
and cargo, the Sea
Knight can also carry
fifteen litters for
casualty evacuation,
plus two medical
attendants.

Right: A US Marine
Corps CH-53E Super
Stallion hovers over
the flight-deck of the
USS Peleliu (LHA 5).
Combat Cargo crew
members are attaching
a forklift to the Sea
Stallion's sling. The
USS Peleliu was part of
Expeditionary Strike
Group One (ESG-1),
which was operating
in the northern
Arabian Sea in
December 2003 while
supporting Operation
Iraqi Freedom.

opposite page, top: CH-53E Super Stallion heavy-lift helicopters conduct low-level flight operations, while Marine AAV7A1 amphibious Attack Vehicles carry out a beach assault. The Super Stallion resulted from a US Marine Corps requirement for greater lifting power than the CH-53 Sea Stallion, which in itself has impressive lift.

opposite page, bottom: The Super Stallion has a maximum speed of 195 mph and a service ceiling of 18,500 feet. The operational radius with a 20,000-lb payload is 575 miles, and it has a maximum payload of 32,000 lb. Here a CH-53E Super Stallion is being moved to the flight-deck from the hangar bay using the starboard elevator aboard USS *Kearsarge* (LHD 3).

below: The Super Stallion is the only helicopter able to lift such loads as the Marine Corps M-198 howitzer and variants of the Light Armoured Vehicle (LAV). The CH-53 is the largest helicopter in the western world, with a maximum gross weight of 9,000 lb. It is powered by two turbo-shaft engines which each generate 4,380 shp. The flightcrew is three and it has accommodation for 55 fully equipped troops.

Below: An MH-53E Sea Dragon of Helicopter Mine Countermeasures Squadron Fifteen (HM-15) – the 'Blackhawks' – dipping i AQS-14 sonar, used to detect underwater mines, in the Arabian Gulf, November 2003. The MH-Sea Dragon is a mine-counter measures variant of the Super Stallion. It is identifiable by the extra-large sponsons on the lower side of the hull which hous additional fuel. It is used primarily for Airborne Mine Countermeasures (AMCM) but has a secondary role of personnel and cargo transport, capable of carrying 55 troops or a 16-ton payload.

Opposite page, top and bottom: An MH-53E Sea Dragon of the 'Blackhawks' lands aboard the USS *Nimitz* (CVN 68). The *Nim* Strike Group and Carrier Air Wing 11 (CVW-11) were deployed in support of Operation Iraqi Freedom in August 2003. The S Dragon is able to tow a variety of mine-sweeping countermeasures systems such as the Mk-105 mine-sweeping sled, the AQS 14 sonar and the Mk-103 mechanical mine-sweeping system.

Above: A UH-3 Sea King of Helicopter Combat Support Squadron Two (HC-2) – the 'Fleet Angels' – of the USS *Nimitz* (CVN 68) in the Arabian Gulf, June 2003. Th Sea King made its maiden flight in 1959. In its long career it has seen service wi anti-submarine warfare, search and rescue, plane guard, surface surveillance and targeting, and as a maritime utilty helicopter. The Sea King is a twin-engin helicopter with a five-blade main rotor. It has a maximu speed of 165 mph with a service ceiling of 15,000 fee and a range of 730 miles. It weighs 5,600 lb when empty and 21,000 when fully loade

Left: The pilot of a UH-3H Se King from Helicopter Comba Support Squadron Two (HC- flying over the Arabian Gulf during Operation Iraqi Freedom. The Sea King has a crew of four and optional seating for 15 passengers.

Right: The Raytheon T-6A Texan II training aircraft prepares to takes off from Naval Air Station (NAS) Pensacola. This aircraft is set to become the US Navy's primary pilot-training aircraft. It has a top speed of 310 mph and a service ceiling of 35,000 feet. It is 3 ft 4 in. long with a wing span of 33 ft 5 in. Its empty weight is 5,000 lb and its maximum take-off weight is 6,500 lb. The service ceiling is 31,000 feet and it has a maximum range of nearly 1,000 miles.

Below: The US Navy's Silver Fox unmanned aerial vehicle (UAV) weighs 20 lb, is 6-feet long with an 8-foot wingspan. It has a 4-lb payload capacity and can stay aloft for five hours. It is controlled from a laptop computer and is equipped with a variety of cameras. It was used during Operation Iraqi Freedom.

Above: The MV-22 Osprey is still under development, although 360 are planned to be built for the US Marine Corps and at the time of writing at least 48 for the US Navy. The Osprey is a twin-engined, dual-piloted, medium-lift, vertical take-off and landing (VTOL), tilt-rotor aircraft designed for combat support and special-operations missions. The Marine Corps should replace its CH-46E and CH-53D medium-lift helicopters with the Osprey. It is shown here landing on the amphibious-assault ship USS *Bataan* (LHD 5).

Below: The Osprey has a maximum cruising speed of 315 mph and in the helicopter mode, at sea level, 115 mph. The service ceiling is 26,000 feet and it has a maximum range of 1,000 miles with a 10,000-lb payload. The aircraft's normal mission take off weight is 55,000 lb, and it weighs 33,000 lb when empty.